A Note to Parents

DK READERS is a compelling program for beginning readers, designed in conjunction with leading literacy experts, including Dr. Linda Gambrell, Professor of Education at Clemson University. Dr. Gambrell has served as President of the National Reading Conference and the College Reading Association, and has recently been elected to serve as President of the International Reading Association.

Beautiful illustrations and superb full-color photographs combine with engaging, easy-to-read stories to offer a fresh approach to each subject in the series. Each DK READER is guaranteed to capture a child's interest while developing his or her reading skills, general knowledge, and love of reading.

The five levels of DK READERS are aimed at different reading abilities, enabling you to choose the books that are exactly right for your child:

Pre-level 1: Learning to read
Level 1: Beginning to read
Level 2: Beginning to read alone
Level 3: Reading alone
Level 4: Proficient readers

The "normal" age at which a child begins to read can be anywhere from three to eight years old. Adult participation through the lower levels is very helpful for providing encouragement, discussing storylines, and sounding out unfamiliar words.

No matter which level you select, you can be sure that you are helping your child learn to read, then read to learn!

DK

LONDON, NEW YORK, MUNICH,
MELBOURNE, AND DELHI

Series Editor Deborah Lock
U.S. Editor John Searcy
Art Editor Mary Sandberg
Production Georgina Hayworth
Picture Researcher Rob Nunn
DTP Designer Ben Hung
Jacket Designer Mary Sandberg

Reading Consultant
Linda Gambrell, Ph.D.

First American Edition, 2007
07 08 09 10 11 10 9 8 7 6 5 4 3 2 1
Published in the United States by DK Publishing
375 Hudson Street, New York, New York 10014

DK books are available at special discounts when purchased in bulk for
sales promotions, premiums, fund-raising, or educational use.
For details, contact:
DK Publishing Special Markets
375 Hudson Street
New York, New York 10014
SpecialSales@dk.com

A catalog record for this book is available
from the Library of Congress.

ISBN: 978-0-7566-3138-3 (Paperback)
ISBN: 978-0-7566-3141-3 (Hardcover)

Color reproduction by Colourscan, Singapore
Printed and bound in China by L. Rex Printing Co. Ltd.

The publisher would like to thank the following for their kind
permission to reproduce their photographs:
a=above, b=below/bottom, c=center, l=left, r=right, t=top

Alamy Images: blickwinkel 22; Chris Howes/Wild Places
Photography 12-13 (b/g); Renee Morris 31b; James Osmond 8-9 (b/g);
Maximilian Weinzierl 19bl. **Ardea:** Pascal Goetgheluck 19.
Corbis: Anthony Bannister/Gallo Images 20; Markus Botzek/zefa 7;
Gary W. Carter 21bl, 32bl; Andrew Fox 6cl; Rose Hartman 15tr, 32cl.
DK Images: Bruce Coleman Agency 11; Natural History Museum,
London 26-27; Paul Wilkinson 26t; Jerry Young 24cr, 25br, 30bc,
30br, 31bl, 33. **FLPA:** Ron Austing 28tl; Yva Momatiuk/John
Eastcott/Minden Pictures 14. **Getty Images:** Stone/David Tipling 13t.
Nature Picture Library: Jurgen Freund 17t; Nick Upton 16-17.
OSF: 5t; Bob Gibbons 21. **Photoshot / NHPA:** Anthony Bannister
18tl, 18tr; Laurie Campbell 29br; Stephen Dalton 23clb.
Still Pictures: Fritz Polking 6br. **SuperStock:** age fotostock 15;
Mauritius 5b. **Warren Photographic:** 23br.

All other images © Dorling Kindersley
For further information see: www.dkimages.com

Discover more at
www.dk.com

Contents

DK READERS

BEGINNING
1
TO READ

Animals
at Home

Written by David Lock

DK Publishing

What is your home like?
Is it cozy and dry?
Animal homes are all shapes
and sizes.
They keep animals and
their babies safe and warm.

hermit crab shell

rabbit warren

stork nest

Some animals build
their own homes.
Many birds make nests.
Some use mud, twigs, or grass.

Weaver-bird
nest

Ovenbird
nest

Others peck out holes in trees.
They build their homes using
only their beaks.

Thousands of termites work together to build a home. Their mound is very strong and it can be very tall.

8

Inside, the tunnels lead to many arch-shaped rooms.

food stores

nursery

Paper wasps collect wood
and chew it into a pulp.
The wasps then use this pulp
to make their nest.

The queen
wasp lays
her eggs inside
the nest's
six-sided cells.

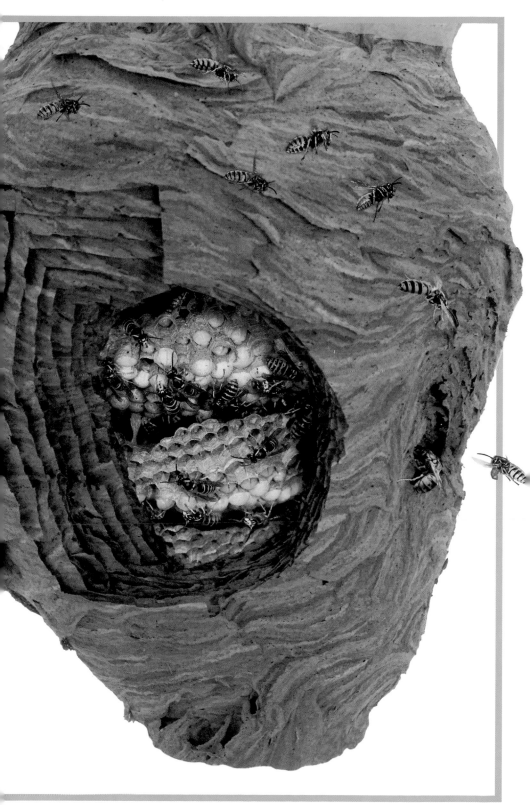

Some animals burrow
under the ground.
Moles dig their tunnels using
their sharp front claws.
They push the soil away,
making hills above the ground.
They eat the worms and insects
that fall into their tunnels.

Beavers build their homes
by weaving sticks together
with their feet.
Their large homes are
called lodges.
The beavers get in and
out of the lodge through
an underwater entrance.

lodge

Some animals live in shells.
Tortoises and snails can
curl up inside their shells.
The shells get bigger as
the animals grow.

shell

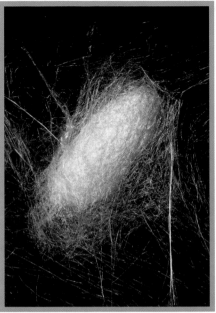

Some insects, like silk moths, make their own silk threads. They weave the silk around themselves to make cocoons. Their homes keep them safe as they change shape and grow wings.

cocoons

19

Spiders can make silk, too.
They use it to make their homes.
Some spiders make webs.
They eat the insects that get
stuck to the strong, sticky silk.
Other spiders build silk-lined
burrows with a hidden trapdoor.

Trapdoor-spider burrow

web

21

Honeybees make beeswax
in their bodies.
They use it to make
their beehive.

There are many six-sided cells
inside the hive.
Honey is stored in some cells.
The bees' young live in others.

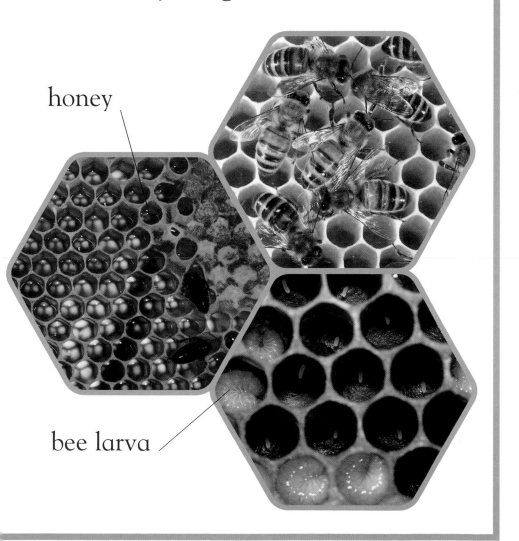

honey

bee larva

Piles of leaves, rotting logs,
and compost heaps may not
seem like good places
to make a home.

beetle

hedgehog

But many small animals feed and
live in these warm, damp places.

ant

toad

Starfish, crabs, and some small fish make their homes in tide pools.

They live in the water that
collects between the rocks
on the seashore.
Shellfish and anemones cling
to the rocks.

limpet

anemone

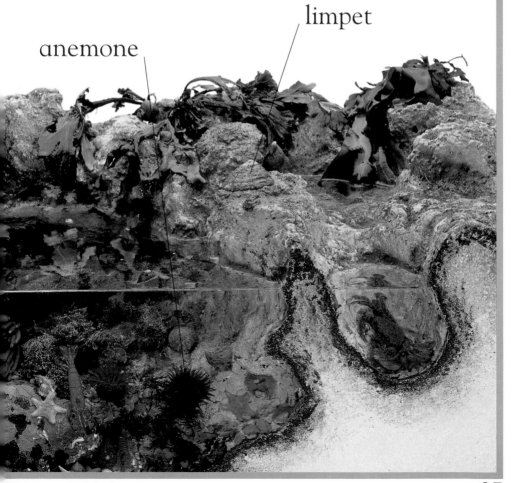

Trees are homes for
many animals.
Birds make nests
in the branches.
Squirrels build homes
called dreys in
the tree trunk.

drey

Insects live in the bark or on the leaves.

Badgers build burrows called setts among the roots.

We are not the only ones who
live in our dry, cozy houses.
Bats may sleep in the attic.
Tiny bugs live in the carpets
and the furniture.
We all want a warm home with
food nearby.

McLEAN COUNTY UNIT #5
105-CARLOCK

Glossary

Cocoon
a silk-wrapped case
made by an insect

Drey
a squirrel's nest

Lodge
a beaver's home

Shell
a hard covering on
an animal's back

Web
a spider's home,
made from its silk

Index